LABRADOR RETRIEVER

The breed

Surprisingly, the ubiquitous Labrador is not a very old breed. The first Labrador breed club was founded in the UK in 1916, and the Yellow Labrador Club was founded in 1925. Labradors were first used as gundogs, collecting and retrieving game that had been shot or wounded. But because of its excellent and companionable temperament, the breed has developed into one of the world's best all-round dogs. Labradors have now assumed all kinds of different roles including assistance dogs, guide dogs for the blind, and sniffer dogs. They are also one of the world's most popular dogs.

The information and recommendations in this book are given without any guarantees on behalf of the author and publisher, who disclaim any liability with the use of this material.

Published by
Interpet Publishing,
Vincent Lane, Dorking,
Surrey, RH4 3YX, UK.

ISBN 978 1 84286 245 2

Printed and bound in China

Contents

1 ABOUT THE LABRADOR

The popular belief is that the Labrador originated on the coast of Newfoundland, Canada, where the explorer John Cabot saw fishermen (who had come to the area from England's Devon and Dorset) using a dog of similar appearance to retrieve fish. The dogs swam out in the icy water to retrieve fish that had escaped from the fishermen's nets, and then pulled the nets in. They also pulled sledges laden with dried fish. These dogs may have come from England with the fishermen (in which case it is suggested that they may have been related to the St. Hubert Hound), or may have been related to the local Newfoundland breed, the St. Johns Water Dog. The white chest, feet, chin, and muzzle

EARLY ANCESTORS

It is thought that the first ancestors of the modern Labrador came from Newfoundland in Canada. In this bleak and inhospitable landscape, the local fisherman relied heavily on their dogs to help them in the fishing trade. Their amazingly dense coats helped them to survive in the icy water and their fantastic ability to retrieve became invaluable.

RIGHT: *The Labrador has brown or hazel eyes, expressing intelligence and good temper.*

known as tuxedo markings – that are characteristic of the St. John's Dog often appear in modern Lab cross-bred dogs and will occasionally manifest in pure-bred Labradors as a small white spot on the chest (which is known as a medallion) or in stray white hairs on the feet or muzzle. Either way, modern Labradors are certainly excellent water dogs, and their weather-resistant coats and unique, otter-like tail, emphasise this trait. Some of these St. John's dogs were brought back to Poole, England in the early nineteenth century and became highly prized sporting dogs, which were used for hunting waterfowl. It was at this time that they became known as "Labradors," to differentiate them from the larger Newfoundland breed. The dogs became popular with various members of the gentry, including the Duke of Buccleuth. He and two other notable patrons of the breed, Colonel Peter

ABOVE: *The webbed toes of the Labrador Retriever make them excellent swimmers.*

Hawker and the Earl of Malmesbury established a breeding programme for the breed and bred several iconic dogs, including Buccleuch Avon and Malmesbury Tramp. These animals are credited with being the forefathers of the modern Labrador.

Hawker eloquently described the breed in his 1812 book *Instructions to Young Sportsmen* as being "by far the best dog for any kind of shooting. He is generally black and no bigger than a Pointer, very fine in legs, with short, smooth hair and does not carry his tail so much curled as the other; is extremely quick, running, swimming and fighting....and their sense of smell is hardly to be credited...." The first painting of Labrador appeared in 1823. Entitled *Cora, A Labrador Bitch* was painted by the distinguished animal artist, Edwin Landseer.

The original Labradors were black, and this is still a popular Labrador colour. But as the breed became more established, different types also became accepted. (Yellow and chocolate puppies had originally been put down.) Ben of Hyde was the first officially recognised yellow Labrador, born in 1899. Golden Labradors were given their own breed club in 1925 and became gradually creamier in colour. Chocolate Labradors became quite popular in the 1930s. Within the breed, dogs bred for different activities have different builds. Labradors bred for showing tend to be shorter legged and heavy while dogs bred for field sports have longer legs and a more athletic physique. Fox red and darker yellow dogs became more popular in the 1980s and several dogs were instrumental in this trend, including the famous sire Balrion King Frost. Although he was a black Labrador, his offspring were often very dark yellow (a shade of butterscotch) or fox red.

Labradors are now the most popular pedigree dog in both Britain and the United States. They took over the position of the most popular dog in 1991. In America, the Labrador took over poll position from the Cocker Spaniel.

BELOW: *The short dense coat allows the Labrador to work in harsh, wet conditions.*

ABOVE: *Labradors work in drug and explosive detection, search and rescue, therapy, assistance, and as retrievers for hunters.*

ABOVE: *Golden Labradors were first recognized in 1899, having their own breed club in 1925.*

THE SHOOTING COMPANION

It was the continual trade between the fishermen of Newfoundland and the ports of the South West coast of Britain that first brought the Newfoundland forebears of the Labrador to Britain. James Harris, the Second Earl of Malmesbury (1778 to 1841) was a prominent aristocrat, politician, and a Member of Parliament. His family home was near the port of Poole in Dorset, and it was here that he first saw and admired the Newfoundland fishing dogs for their remarkable retrieving abilities. He was quick to realize how useful they would be as gun dogs. Malmesbury and Colonel Peter Hawker bought several dogs from the Canadian fishermen and instituted a breeding programme that ultimately resulted in the modern Labrador.

It is the Labrador's ability to work quietly alongside hunters, while watching for shot birds to fall from the sky and marking where they land, then using their sensitive nose to find and retrieve dead or wounded birds which has made them the best retrievers.

Recognition at last

It was not only the Earl of Malmesbury, The Duke of Buccleuch, and Colonel Peter Hawker that were responsible for the establishment of the Labrador as a recognizable breed. The Honorable Arthur Holland-Hibbert (1855 to 1935), who inherited the title of the Third Viscount Knutsford on the death of his elder twin brother Sydney in 1931 also made a great contribution. Holland-Hibbert became very interested in the new breed and became an enthusiastic Labrador owner. He also bred his dogs and established a reputation for his well-known Munden kennel. His strain was notable for producing a line of healthy and enterprising Labradors. Holland-Hibbert was also highly instrumental in gaining recognition for the breed from the British Kennel Club. The first seven Labradors registered with the club were from the Munden Kennels and his dog, Munden Single was the first Labrador to run in a Field Trial.

Building on this foundation of sound breeding, the modern Labrador has been able to become one of the most successful and versatile dog breeds. Not only are Labradors blessed with an easy-going and playful temperament that means that they make wonderful pets, but their adaptability and eagerness to please means that they have become invaluable to their human owners in many different roles.

INFLUENTIAL DOGS

Buccleuch Avon was one of the most important ancestors of the modern Labrador. He is also credited with being the forebear of all black Labradors. The dog was actually bred by the Earl of Malmesbury. Born in 1885, he was the son of Malmesbury Tramp and a bitch called June. Along with two other puppies, Malmesbury gifted the dog to his shooting companion, the Sixth Duke of Buccleuch.

Buccleuch used the dog as the foundation of the world-renowned Buccleuch Kennel and it is said that all the dogs from this kennel can trace their lineage straight back to the original dogs from Newfoundland. They are notorious for their good nose, tender mouth and courageous temperaments. They also have the breed's true thick double coat and are invariably black.

2 DOG OR PUPPY?

Once you have decided that you would like a Labrador to share your life, the next big decision you will need to make is if you would be better off getting a puppy or a grown-up dog. This is an important choice that could affect your family for years to come. Many people think that if they get a puppy, it will be a completely blank canvas, and they will be able to shape it into the dog they want. This is largely true, but you will need to make sure that

ABOVE AND BELOW: *A Labrador has a life span of over 10 years and will need about 2 hours exercise a day.*

ABOVE: *See both parents if you can when selecting a puppy.*

you get a dog from a reliable strain and it would be wise to see both parents and check that they both have happy temperaments.

You also need to make sure that a puppy would fit into your family and working life. It is very difficult to bring up a puppy unless someone is at home during the day to house train the puppy, keep him out of trouble, and keep him company. Puppies need constant supervision and this might also be difficult if you have young children that also need a lot of attention. However, Labradors are usually very tolerant of young children and toddlers and they can both benefit from growing up together, although all young children need to be taught to respect animals so that they don't tease the puppy and get a bad reaction.

Inevitably, the first few days with a puppy are pretty tiring, until you have established a good routine. You will need to comfort him, as he may well be missing his mother and littermates. You will need to start to house train him, and clear up accidents as calmly as possible. You will also need to keep your new puppy safe by pup-proofing your home and garden.

The older dog

One of the great things about adopting a grown-up Labrador is that you are probably giving a home to a dog that really needs one. There will also be advantages to you, your older dog may well be house trained (or nearly house trained!) and may also have been taught how to walk on the lead, and ride in the car. You can also see exactly what you are getting in the way of temperament and size. The best way to find an older Labrador may be through a breed rescue organization. Dogs can end up in rescue kennels for many reasons most of which are not any fault of the dog. For example, his owner may have died or become ill. One of the great things about Labradors is because they are such people-loving dogs, they will soon adapt to you and your lifestyle. An older dog might also find it easier if you are not at home all day and probably won't be as needy as a puppy. Kennel owners may also have slightly older dogs for re-homing. Dogs that haven't made it as show dogs or bitches that have passed the age of breeding may become available and would hugely benefit from a relaxing home of their own. Older people may also feel that a more mature dog would be less likely to trip them up or push them over, and won't be too boisterous around the home. If you think your oldie

ABOVE: *Owners may prefer an older dog who is less boisterous.*

ABOVE: *The male Labrador Retriever tends to be larger and heavier than the female of the breed.*

has behaviour problems, take him to training lessons right away.

The other way to obtain an older dog is through a Labrador Retriever rescue scheme (your local breed club secretary will have details).

A MALE OR FEMALE?

The personality differences between male and female Labradors are quite subtle, and both make excellent pets and hunting partners. Many potential Labrador owners are under the impression that Labrador dogs are likely to roam from home. This is not actually the case. Labradors are not very prone to wanderlust, but bitches are more likely to have an independent streak. Of course, it is up to you as the owner to make sure that your dog is safely confined. Bitches may also be more stubborn and territorial and can be moody when they are in season. The other benefit of dogs is that you won't have to cope with their seasons every six months, unless you have your bitch spayed. Male Labradors are usually slightly larger and heavier than bitches, and can be more exuberant. But they almost always have great characters and are very trainable, as well as being loving and faithful. (Sometimes males can be a little bit too protective, but this is usually resolved if your dog is neutered.) Bitches can also be a little more demanding, and have their own agendas.

Labrador colours

DOES COLOUR MAKE A DIFFERENCE?

Labradors come in a range of attractive colours, and each of these has its adherents. Labrador coats can be wholly black, yellow or chocolate (also known as liver). "Yellow" can range all the way from light cream to fox red. It is quite possible to view a litter where puppies of all three colours are available. The British Kennel Club breed standard states that a small white spot on the chest is also permissible. Coat colour is the only difference between these dogs, as they are the same size and weight and have the same texture of coat. One of the things to consider is that, as all Labradors moult, which colour will show up worst on your furnishings? Some people claim that black Labradors make the best retrievers, but this is definitely not the case. The coat colour of your dog will make no difference to his training. But when you are buying a Labrador you should spend more effort checking that his health and genetic heritage are sound rather than worry about the colour of his coat. One of the few colour considerations that might be a factor is that, if you want to

LEFT: *Labradors come in black, yellow, or chocolate.*

ABOVE: *An adaptable dog, he comes into his own in rural surroundings.*

breed from your dog, it is quite difficult for an inexperienced breeder to keep the coat and skin pigment of chocolate dogs true into future generations. Generally speaking, colour preference is not a good reason to choose a dog. You should always concentrate on the temperament and good health of your potential soul mate. The Labrador is prone to three genetic diseases and your major preoccupation should be to avoid buying a pet with a known history of any of these diseases. These conditions are central progressive retinal atrophy, hip dysplasia, and osteochondrosis.

Responsible breeding is now trying to eradicate these conditions from the Labrador breed.

FINDING A BREEDER

You should always buy your Labrador from a recognized breeder. The Kennel Club has a list of these. Good Labrador breeders will check the health of their breeding stock, ensuring that their hips are scored and their eyes are tested. The breeder should be able to show you a certificate that these tests have been done.

Assessing the puppies

Once you have found a litter from which to choose your puppy you need to use some objectivity to choose the right dog for you. In fact, there's no point in looking at a litter prior to five weeks of age. You need to see the puppies on their feet before you can judge them properly. If possible, it would be great to see the puppies' mother and father. The main points to look for are your puppy's physical and behavioural health. So far as his physical health goes, there are several things that you should look out for.

WAITING FOR YOUR PUPPY

Once you have chosen your Labrador puppy, it would be great if you could go back to the breeder to visit him and start the bonding process as soon as possible. You can also keep an eye on him to make sure that he stays in good health before you pick him up. This should be at around eight weeks old. A good breeder will be happy to welcome you to see your puppy and will be pleased by your interest.

The puppy should have a good level of energy, and appear alert and interested in his surroundings. His eyes should be bright and clear without any crust or discharge, and he should be able to see a ball that rolls by slowly. He should look well fed, and have a little fat over his ribs. A healthy puppy's bottom should be free from faeces. His coat

BELOW: *Sometimes a puppy will seem to choose you!*

should be glossy and not scurfy, dull or greasy. He should be able to walk freely without any limping or discomfort. The puppy should be able to hear you if you clap behind his head.

So far as his behaviour goes, you should look for a puppy that seems to be interacting well with his littermates - playing nicely without being too assertive. The puppy should also be interested in playing with you and should approach you willingly. He should be happy about being handled, and let you cuddle him and touch him all over his body. If he remains calm and relaxed while you do this, he is likely to be easier to handle when he grows up.

PUPPY LAYETTE

You will need to equip yourself with some simple pup-friendly equipment before you go and collect your Labrador. Here is a quick checklist:

- Bed, basket, or dog crate
- Puppy collar and lead
- Grooming brush
- Safe, durable puppy-friendly toys
- Puppy food (as per the breeder's instructions)

BELOW: *Your chosen puppy should have a good level of energy.*

Feeding your puppy

Most breeders will give you a diet sheet that should cover the first six months of your puppy's life. This will mean that you can keep the continuity of his diet which will mean one less change for him to cope with, and prevent any unnecessary stress. Many breeders will give you some of the food they are feeding the puppy for the first couple of days. Give your puppy a small meal when you first bring him home, although he may be too nervous or tired to eat at first. You may wish to adjust your new puppy's diet in time, but you should introduce new foods to his diet over a period of time. A puppy's stomach is quite delicate and can be upset by an abrupt change in his feeding regime. You will need at least two shallow-sided bowls for the puppy, one for food and one for water. Stainless steel bowls are ideal as they are both clean and unbreakable.

COLLECTING YOUR PUPPY

Its a good idea to take someone with you when you go to collect your Labrador puppy, so that one of you can drive and the other one can comfort the pup. A towel to mop up any accidents is a good idea. When you collect him, make sure that you find out when he will need his next worming treatment and what vaccinations he has had. You should also receive a copy of your puppy's pedigree.

ABOVE: *A dog crate is useful when you travel with your Labrador Retriever.*

Bringing your puppy home

Although it is a very exciting time when you bring your Labrador home for the first time, you should try to keep the atmosphere as calm and reassuring as possible. Moving to his new home is a complete change for your puppy and he has to fit into a completely new environment. Alternatively, if you are bringing an older dog into your home, he may already have insecurities that you will need to allay.

LIFE CHANGES

Your puppy will have a lot of things to adjust to. At first, he may well feel lonely. A hot water bottle wrapped up in a blanket and a cuddly toy may help. Beware of going to your puppy if he cries during his first night with you. This is giving him the message that you will come running whenever he cries. You may also be tempted to take a miserable puppy into your own bed which you may not want to do in the long-term.

If you are re-homing an older dog, be sure to call him by the name he is used to. Trying to change it to something you prefer will confuse him utterly.

LEFT: *If you are buying an older dog, he will feel unsure of his new surroundings.*

3 GENERAL CARE

Now that you have brought your Labrador puppy home, it's your responsibility to make sure that he grows up to be a healthy and happy dog. Good nutrition is one of the cornerstones of the care that he will need from you.

PUPPY NUTRITION

If you have bought your dog from a responsible breeder, they should have given you a diet sheet to follow. If you don't know what your puppy has been eating you will need to buy him some suitable puppy food. These foods are now sometimes breed specific. If you buy dry food, you need to make very sure that your puppy has access to water at all times, as these foods can make your dog very thirsty. A common mistake made by Labrador owners is to give their puppies cows' milk. This can badly upset your puppy's stomach and give him diarrhoea. Fully-weaned puppies don't need milk of any kind, but if you really want to give him milk, most puppies can tolerate either fresh or dried goats' milk.

As your puppy only has a small tummy, you will need to divide your puppy's food into several small meals. Four meals are usually considered best for puppies up to the age of twelve weeks old; breakfast, lunch, tea, and supper. Serving meals at 7a.m., 11a.m., 3p.m. and 7p.m. works quite well. Don't allow him to go without food for more than six hours in the day. Leave his food down for around ten minutes so that he learns to eat up reasonably quickly. Don't worry if he doesn't finish his food at this age, he may just be full. Dried food will swell in the puppy's tummy and he will soon feel satisfied.

ABOVE: *Labradors are well known for their tremendous appetites.*

REFRIGERATED FOOD

Food from the refridgerator should be warmed to room temperature before feeding time.

Leaving his food down for him to graze on is not very salubrious. At this age, intervals of three to four hours between his meals should be about right. Once your puppy is three months old, he can move to three meals a day. By the time he is six months old, two daily meals will be sufficient. When your dog reaches his first birthday, you can move to a single daily meal if you like, but many people prefer to divide their dog's food into two meals a day. If you are unhappy feeding a complete dry diet, you can always supplement this with some tasty treats, such as a little grated cheese or an egg.

Most Labradors have great appetites, and you shouldn't struggle to get your puppy eating heartily. Although complete diets are extremely convenient, and contain everything your puppy needs, some owners prefer a more traditional puppy diet of various nutritious foods including baby porridge, eggs, meat, baby rusks, egg custard, and rice pudding. This is a lot more work! It is very unlikely that household scraps will provide enough nutrition for your puppy to grow up strong and healthy.

In recent years, some Labrador owners have moved over to the method of "raw" feeding where dogs are fed on raw meat and bones.

ABOVE: *Diet is extremely important for your puppy's healthy development to adulthood.*

TRADITIONAL PUPPY DIET

- **Breakfast** Porridge made with warm milk and baby cereal, or brown bread soaked in warm milk. You can mix a raw egg in with this mixture a couple of times a week. You can also mix vitamin supplements into this meal.

- **Lunch:** 170 to 225g of raw, chopped beef mixed with 60 to 85g of soaked puppy biscuits. This needs to be a good-quality wholemeal biscuit.
- **Afternoon Snack:** A snack of baby rusks, baked egg custard, or half a can of rice pudding.
- **Supper:** This should be the same food and quantity offered at lunchtime.
- **Bedtime:** Most puppies appreciate a small biscuit to go to bed with.

This diet is effective, but very time-consuming. Most people have now changed over to a variant of the modern diet opposite.

MODERN PUPPY DIET

Always supply water for your dog.

- **Breakfast** 110 to 170g of pre-soaked, complete food. You should make sure that you choose a good-quality brand of complete diet. Your puppy's breeder may be able to advise you.
- **Lunch:** 140 to 280ml of powdered or fresh goat's milk can be added to porridge.
- **Tea:** The same meal as served at breakfast time.
- **Supper** (but no later than 7p.m.): The same meal served at lunch. Don't feed your puppy any later than about 7 p.m. as this may make it difficult for him to get through the night without relieving himself.
- **Last thing at night:** Your puppy will enjoy a small biscuit to go to bed with.

As well as being convenient and clean, another benefit of feeding a complete dry dog food to your puppy is that, when he grows up, you can give him the adult version of the same diet.

BELOW: *As your dog matures, he can be switched to an adult version of the diet.*

Reducing feeds

SWIMMING BOWL

If you feed your Labrador puppy with complete dry food, you should make absolutely sure that they have access to plenty of fresh water at all times. Labrador puppies are notorious for splashing around in their water bowls, so you need to double check that they haven't spilt it all.

LEFT: *You can reduce your puppy's meals to two a day at six months of age.*

Your puppy will quickly grow through several developmental stages in his first year, and his nutritional intake must keep pace with this. As he grows older, you can start reducing the number of feeds he is offered, and increase the quantity he eats at each meal. At about twelve weeks, you can start to drop one of the milk feeds, and eliminate the afternoon snack. To compensate for this you should offer more meat and biscuits at the other feeds. You should start to stop the other milk feed when your puppy is around six months old, aiming to eliminate it by the age of eight months.

By the time your Labrador reaches nine months old, he can be reduced to just one daily meal, and a biscuit to eat at bed time. He should consume around 680g of complete dry food, or 450g of meat with 225 to 340g of dry food a day. You can determine the most convenient time of day for your dog to receive his meal.

Worming

All dogs have worms at some point in their lives, and puppies are at the most risk from infestation. Worms are passed from the mother even before birth and through their milk. They then live in the puppy's intestine and feed on partly digested food. Untreated worms can cause serious illnesses in puppies, including weight loss, vomiting, diarrhoea, a swollen tummy, and even death. An infested puppy cannot get the benefit from his food and will not thrive. He may also cough and his coat may look dull. Puppies need regular worming to combat this and should be wormed from two weeks of age at two weekly intervals until they are twelve weeks of age, then every month until they are six months of age. Worming should continue at least three times a year with a recommended veterinary preparation for the rest of the dog's life. Dogs are prone to two main types of worms, tapeworms and roundworms. Roundworms can appear like elastic bands, up to several inches in length. Tapeworms can appear like white grains of rice, which are joined together to form a tape. These are most commonly found in adult dogs and very rarely in puppies.

Your breeder should tell you about the worming programme they have been using, and when the next treatment is due. It may be a good plan to let your puppy settle down before you worm him. Twelve weeks is usually considered to be a good age for this. Your vet can recommend a good product to use. Roundworms are spread through the environment while tapeworms are commonly spread by fleas, so it is wise to treat an infested dog for flea infestation. Climate change has meant that dogs are now subject to new types of worm, Angiostrongylus, for example. These worms can live in the lungs or in the major blood vessels and may even cause death. Ordinary worming medicine does not work against these parasites.

ABOVE: *All dogs must be treated for worms or they will not get the full benefit from their food.*

Vaccinations

One of the most important things you need to do for your Labrador puppy is to make sure that he is enrolled into a comprehensive vaccination programme. This will protect him against the serious illnesses of distemper, hepatitis, parvovirus, leptospirosis, and kennel cough. He will need regular boosters throughout his life. You should keep your puppy at home until he is fully protected.

Puppies should be vaccinated at 6-9 weeks of age and then again at 10-12 weeks. They will usually become fully protected two weeks after the second vaccination but your vet may recommend a third dose for some puppies. The vaccine your vet will use will contain a modified dose of the disease that will stimulate your dog's immune system to produce antibodies that will be able to fight the disease. If your puppy is unwell, it may be a good idea to postpone his injections for a while, to minimise the small risk of adverse reaction. Most vaccines are injected into the scruff, but the kennel cough vaccine is given as drops into the nose. The kennel cough vaccine is usually only given to dogs who will be left in boarding kennels, but it may also be useful if your dog needs to go into hospital for any reason.

When you take your unvaccinated puppy to the vet, you should make sure that you carry him and do not put him down in the surgery.

ABOVE: *Your puppies should not leave the safety of the garden until they are protected by innoculation.*

KEEP A RECORD

If you plan to put your dog into a boarding kennel, you will need to keep an up-to-date card showing the vaccinations he has had.

Exercise

ABOVE: *It is important to keep your Labrador's mind stimulated.*

As your new Labrador puppy comes from a long line of working dogs, he needs to be kept both mentally and physically active to make sure he is stimulated and happy. But it is very important to exercise Labrador puppies in moderation as their bones are still soft and growing. Over-exercising a puppy can lead to damage. This is an especially serious consideration in Labradors, as the breed is prone to hip problems and is particularly important when the status of the hips of the puppy's parents is poor or unknown.

Most experts recommend that Labradors should not be taken on long walks until they are around a year old and suggest around five minutes of exercise per day for every month of the puppy's age. This would mean no more than thirty-five minutes of walking for a seven month old dog per day. By the time he is a year old, he can walk for hours.

You should also try to avoid strenuous and jerky activities at this stage, such as stair climbing, jumping in and out of the car, and on and off furniture.

As your Labrador matures, exercise will become an increasingly important part of his day. Although he will need

ABOVE: *Labradors love water and this can be incorporated into their exercise regime.*

variety. You can also take toys with you on his walk, so that you can play with these as you go. Labradors also love a swim, but you will need to take a towel if you go in the car. When your dog is a veteran, you will need to keep an eye on the amount of exercise he gets. Too much can stress his joints. He may benefit from taking more, shorter walks. Swimming can also help, but a warm hydrotherapy pool will be more beneficial to his joints.

Sleeping arrangements

One of the most important things to decide is where your puppy is going to sleep. This is crucial as this is somewhere that your puppy needs to feel completely safe and secure. It should be a place that suits both you and the dog. The most important thing is that the sleeping area should be warm, dry, and completely draught free. Many owners prefer their new puppies to sleep in the kitchen or utility room as these rooms usually have washable floors. But you should not let him sleep in a confined space where there is a boiler in case of carbon monoxide leaks. You could also fence off a small area so that your puppy won't be able to get into trouble in the night. A playpen would be ideal for this. The floor of the pen could also be covered with newspaper. Although there are many different kinds of dog beds on the market, the simple plastic kidney-shaped baskets, which come in many different sizes and colours, are some of the most practical.

ABOVE: *Few puppies can resist chewing a wicker bed.*

BEWARE!

Make absolutely sure that there are no electrical wires or cables near your puppy's sleeping quarters that he could chew in a bored moment.....

RIGHT: *A pup should feel safe and secure in his sleeping quarters.*

ABOVE: *Labradors like a comfortable place to sleep.*

They resist chewing and can be washed and disinfected. They can also be filled with cosy pads or mattresses on which the puppy can sleep comfortably. These mattress inserts can usually be washed in the washing machine. It's a good idea to buy two of these in case of accidents! Although most puppies are naturally clean in their bed, accidents can happen. An excellent idea is to replace the fabric softener in the washing cycle with a slug of disinfectant to make sure that any germs or bad smells are destroyed. Wicker baskets can be dangerous when chewed as the sharp sticks can damage the puppy's mouth or throat. Equally, bean bag beds can easily be chewed through and the polystyrene beans they contain are difficult to clean up. Polyester bedding strips are ideal. They are warm and comfortable, can be machine-washed, and are difficult to chew.

SLEEP TIGHT!

Young puppies should be allowed to sleep and rest as much as they want, so they need to have their bed positioned away from the noisy centre of your home. A puppy should never be woken up to play with, and this should be explained to any children in the house! You should encourage your puppy to spend some quiet time resting alone. As for babies, sleep is crucial to your puppy's normal development. A puppy will sleep better at night if he has company, so you might like to consider having his bed in your bedroom, or on the landing outside your room (with your door open) where he can hear and smell you. Although it can be tempting, it can cause problems later on if you allow your puppy to sleep on your bed with you. You need to remember that your Labrador may grow into a 35kg adult dog, which may make him a large and inconvenient bedfellow. Adult dogs also sleep better in the company of other dogs, animals or humans. Dogs that spend their nights alone may not feel sleepy enough to sleep deeply.

Sleep savvy

ABOVE: *Make the crate a comfy place.*

A normal healthy adult Labrador will sleep or doze in many sessions during the day and night. This will usually add up to between twelve and fourteen hours spent asleep each day. Dogs sleeping more than this can become depressed, while dogs that sleep less than this are likely to be over anxious. The amount of sleep your dog gets directly affects his serotonin levels. The level of serotonin in a dog's brain regulates many aspects of his behaviour, including depression and aggression. This illustrates how important your dog's sleeping conditions are to his general welfare. A dog needs space to sleep on his side with his legs out to achieve full REM sleep. As in humans, REM sleep is essential for processing the day's events and learning from them. It is also important that your Labrador is neither too hot nor cold in his bed.

DOG CRATES

A dog crate is usually a plastic or metal collapsible, enclosed pen that is just large enough for a dog to stand up and turn around. The crate is a place for the dog to be when no one is around to supervise him. It is the dog's bed and sanctuary. Its purpose is to provide confinement for reasons of safety, security for the dog, housetraining, prevention of destructive behaviour, and/or travel. If you use the crate correctly, it can have many advantages for you and your dog. You can enjoy peace of mind when you are out, and your dog can feel safe and secure. Your dog can also travel safely in the crate.

BELOW: *Lure your puppy into the crate with a toy.*

Grooming

Although black Labradors generally do not shed as much as golden Labradors, all Labradors will shed to some extent. A Labrador's coat is a good indicator of his general health and well-being. The happier he is, the glossier his coat will be. Brushing also helps to get rid of the dead coat and brings the new coat through more quickly so that the "shedding" time is kept to a minimum. This is also a good time to check for any problems such as fleas, lumps, bumps, or cuts.

A healthy dog will have a good, glossy coat, and most Labradors love to be brushed. This also helps to bring the new coat back in a little faster when your dog is shedding.

EARS

You can also use the weekly check to keep an eye on your dog's ears. If your

GROOMING TOOLS

The Labrador is a short-coated breed, and so does not require a great deal of grooming. All you will need are the basic tools, such as a good brush and a comb, and a weekly grooming session will be sufficient to keep your dog in good condition.

LEFT: *Early grooming sessions will make brushing easier.*

dog is scratching, shaking his head and holding an ear slightly away from the head, this might mean that your dog has got ear trouble and you need to consult your vet. You can also buy special ear cleaners that help to clear excessive ear wax.

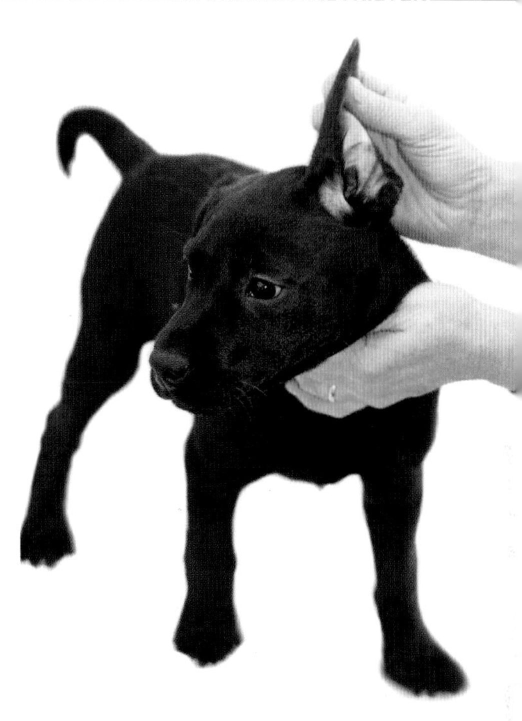

ABOVE: *It's important to keep your Labrador's ears clean.*

NAILS

If you walk your dog on hard surfaces, you may be able to keep his nails short just by doing this. But if you mostly walk your dog in the country, you should budget to clip his nails regularly. If you do this every one or two weeks, you will only need to remove the nail tips to keep them comfortable for him. This will also prevent him developing the splay-footed appearance that Labradors get when their nails are too long. You must take every precaution to avoid cutting into the quick of the nail, as this will be very painful for your dog.

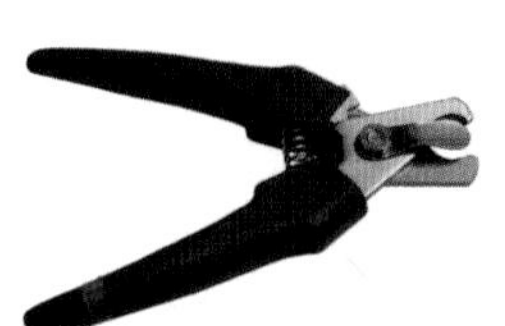

ABOVE: *Nail clippers*

RIGHT: *Your dog's nails will need trimming every other week.*

4 EARLY LEARNING

Almost as soon as you bring your new Labrador puppy home, you should start his basic training. If you want to have a well-behaved and obedient dog, the time and effort you put into your dog at this early stage will pay dividends later on. It will help to make him the kind of dog that is a pleasure to own and to live with.

HOUSE TRAINING

House training is the first sort of training that you should begin with your puppy. It should begin as soon as you first arrive home with him. With vigilance and positive training methods, most puppies quickly learn how to be clean in the house. Being a highly intelligent breed, Labradors are particularly quick to learn.

House training will be easier if your puppy has a settled routine, sleeping and eating at the same times during the day. Puppies usually need to relieve themselves when they wake up, during play, and after meals. You should also watch for signs indicating that your puppy wants to

ABOVE: *Your pup will learn to trust you and feel safe when you take him out.*

go to the toilet; restlessness, whining, tail raising, sniffing, and circling around. You should take your puppy to the same place in the garden on each of these occasions. You should encourage him with a consistent phrase such as "toilet." As soon as the puppy performs, you should praise him and play with him. You may be surprised how often your puppy needs to relieve himself, but remember he has only a small bladder at this age.

A puppy should never be chastised for making "mistakes." Instead, you should say a firm "no" to the puppy and take him outside to his toilet area. You then need to clean up well so that no smell lingers. This might give the puppy the idea that he can use that spot for his "business" in the future. Remember that your puppy will not have full bladder control until he is about four months old and should never be punished for making mistakes.

PUPPY TRAINING

Labrador pups enjoy learning new tricks and skills. Early training allows owners to capitalise on their pet's receptive and confident young mind. If your puppy came from a good home, he will be used to being handled. This is very important and you should make sure that you get him used to being groomed; having his nails clipped, teeth cleaned, and ears checked and cleaned. This will prevent a lot of heartache later on. Small puppies are usually very compliant and will soon get used to this treatment. This handling will become invaluable if you decide to train your dog for a job or work, or to show him. Remember that a puppy has a lot to learn in his first few months, but one of the most important lessons is to socialize him with humans and other animals. If you are firm and loving with him, he will come to know what you expect. The golden rule is to praise him when he is good and ignore him when he is naughty! If you have a good bond with your puppy, he will trust you and want to please you by obeying your wishes. His faith in you will also reassure him when he is confused by new situations.

ABOVE: *Be consistent with your rules.*

Lead-training

ABOVE: *Reassure your puppy when you first take him out on the lead.*

Most Labradors very quickly learn how to walk on the lead. Their natural inclination is to keep close to you so attaching a lead is usually no problem. Twelve to fourteen weeks is a good age for a puppy to start wearing his first collar. The puppy's neck will be very soft and delicate so you should use a very soft and comfortable collar. Your puppy will soon grow out of this, so wait until he is at least six months of age before you buy him anything expensive.

ABOVE: *If your dog is used to handling it will make it easier to take him out.*

ABOVE: *A soft collar is ideal for your puppy.*

The best place to begin training your puppy is in your garden. In this safe and controlled environment, your puppy can learn about walking on the lead where there is nothing to upset or distract him. Encourage him and praise him as he walks well, but do not allow him to rush forwards and pull. If he does, keep calm and talk to him, then persuade him to walk a few steps, then praise again. It will not take long for him to learn. Calm lead work will build a strong bond of trust between you so that when he goes out into the world and meets new and scary things he will look to you for reassurance.

ABOVE: *Make sure the collar lets you slip two fingers inside it.*

ABOVE: *Wearing a collar all the time will spoil the fur if you show your dog later.*

Most Labradors are easy to train to walk on the lead. If you maintain a calm, patient and confident approach, it will click all the quicker! To get your Labrador puppy to accept the lead, it is helpful if you can train them to be comfortable in their collar first. This should be a comfortable fit, snug so that it can't get caught on anything, but not so tight so that the puppy can feel it. The best thing is for it to be so comfortable that the puppy can forget about it completely. You can then attach the lead to the collar when he is already engaged with a pleasant activity, such as eating his food. If your puppy starts to scratch at the collar, distract him until he stops, maybe by offering a treat. Once he has accepted that you have attached the lead to the collar, try to get him to follow you by carrying something that you know your pup likes, such as a toy or a biscuit. Make sure that you apply no pressure to the lead and certainly don't pull on the lead to get him to come to you, or walk to heel.

ABOVE: *A perfectly trained Labrador.*

BELOW: *Your pup may need some encouragement to walk on the lead.*

LITTLE AND OFTEN

Make sure that you have got your puppy's attention before you give a command. You should aim only to give commands that your puppy obeys, so you need to make sure that he is engaged with you. You can do this by calling his name, or snapping your fingers until you have good eye contact with him. Then give your command, and make sure that your puppy follows through. Give him time to respond but ensure that he does as you have asked. Don't keep repeating the command as this means that your pup chooses when he obeys you. The idea is that he should obey you at once.

Puppy's have only a short attention span, so you should keep your training sessions to no more than five or ten minutes. He won't be able to focus for much longer than this. It's important to keep the atmosphere of the training sessions as positive as possible, with lots of praise. If your puppy seems confused by a new command, go back to something you know he can do so that you can end the session on a positive note. If you are using training treats as part of your method, you may well find that it's better to time your sessions before meals, when the puppy might be a little hungry. But as your puppy gradually learns your commands, you should phase out the treats. Labradors have a tendency to put on weight, so you don't want to have to rely on treats in the long term.

ABOVE: *Puppies can be trained from the moment you own them.*

RIGHT: *Firstly you get his attention with a treat in your hand. Then you slowly move it back up and over his head.*

TEACHING THE SIT

Teaching your puppy to sit is a useful exercise, as it shows him that you are in control. It can also calm a difficult situation. Most Labradors will sit naturally just by voice. If, however, your puppy does not understand, repeat the command "sit" and gently push the puppy's hindquarters down into the sitting position and then reward with a treat. The puppy will learn quickly.

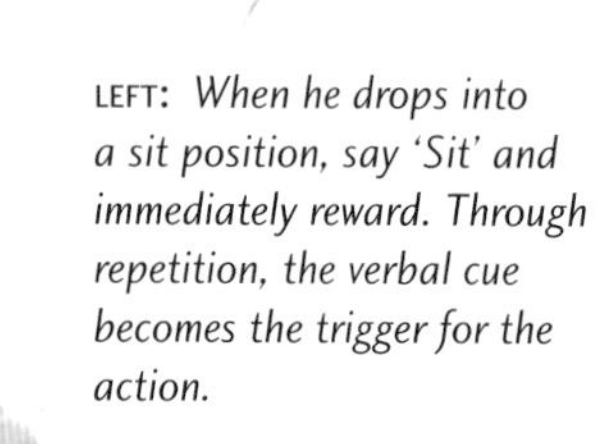

LEFT: *When he drops into a sit position, say 'Sit' and immediately reward. Through repetition, the verbal cue becomes the trigger for the action.*

RIGHT: *Teaching the Down is the next step in your puppy's training.*

TEACHING THE DOWN

The Down is the next command after Sit. Start with your puppy at the Sit position. Have a treat in your hand which you then hold on the floor in front of the puppy. When the puppy goes down for it give the command "Down" followed by the reward and praise. When this exercise is repeated several times the puppy will go down without you having to put your hand to the floor, but reward and praise every time until it is firmly established. If the puppy will not go down at the start of this training, you can give very gentle pressure on the forequarters to encourage him to go down to the floor.

ABOVE: *First teach the Stay with your dog on his lead.*

TEACHING THE STAY

Learning to "Stay" is important to all dogs. When you first start to teach your puppy to stay, it is best to have him on the lead. Ask the puppy to either sit, or go down, with the lead extended from you to the puppy; walk away backwards (facing the puppy) and repeat the command "Stay". When you get as far as the end of the lead, stand still for a few seconds, ask the puppy to come, and praise him. Gradually lengthen the distance you leave the puppy and always give praise when he does it right. If the puppy breaks the Stay, take him back to where you left him at Sit or Down and repeat the exercise, but do not go so far away from him before you call him. This exercise will take time and patience; little and often is best. It may be helpful if you use a hand signal as well as the command.

ABOVE: *Remember your dog will respond to your body language as well as your voice.*

TEACHING RECALL

Start to teach your puppy his name as soon as you get him and use it all the time, especially at meal times and when you give him a treat. Train him to come to you by calling his name and rewarding him when he comes to you with a cuddle or treat. This will soon become second nature to him. Coming when called is important for your dog's future safety and for your peace of mind so imprint it into his mind at an early age.

WAIT!

The Stay exercise and the Recall exercise should be separated in your dog's mind, and so it is easier to use a different command, i.e. "Wait", when you are doing a Recall.

ABOVE: *Crouch down to your puppy's level and call him to you.*

LEFT: *Train him to come to you by calling his name.*

BELOW: *Don't get too intense when you start training. Give your dog plenty of breaks and time to rest.*

A good idea is to carry a treat in a crinkly paper bag. If your puppy doesn't come on command, you can rustle the bag while you repeat the command. As soon as he has made the connection between the rustling paper and the treat, he will always come to you. When he does, you should stroke and praise him.

If your Labrador decides to disobey you, use a low growly voice to get his attention. Once you have it, you should immediately change your tone to a soft and encouraging tone and call him again. This should do the trick. When he has obeyed you, give him a treat and praise him. You should also remember that however angry your dog has made you by refusing to come when he has been called, you must never punish him when does finally come to you. This will confuse him utterly and undermine his trust in your leadership.

Your puppy at six months

How you bring up your Labrador retriever puppy for the first six months will have a great impact on the quality of dog that you end up with. Frequent human contact and exposure to a variety of different surroundings is very important. Most Labradors live in the house with their owners, and this is a good way to maintain a good level of contact. By the time he is six months old, your puppy should have grasped the basics of his training. He should be clean in the house, trained to the lead, and come when he is called. Of course, you may also want to train him to be a retriever! In these early months, play retrieves are an excellent activity but must be strictly limited to two to three brief sessions a day so that your dog develops an intense desire to retrieve. Throwing a rolled-up flannel down a hallway is an excellent way to start developing the right habits. With any training do remember that your young puppy has a short attention span. Frequent short sessions are best. Remember that repetition and consistency work best and are so much more effective than punishment or bribes.

RIGHT: *your Labrador is likely to become bored if he is left completely to his own devices.*

5 FURTHER TRAINING

Most Labrador Retrievers fall into one of two different categories, working (field or gun) dogs, or show (bench) dogs. Even if you only want a pet or companion animal, you will need to choose between them. Both kinds of Labrador have different characteristics and personalities. Working Labradors are highly intelligent and are usually easier to train, even for an inexperienced owner. They are often very sensitive animals that live to please their owners. Less positively, this sensitivity can sometimes lead to excessive nervousness. This can usually be offset by making sure that you socialize your puppy at an early age. More negatively, working Labradors often have strong hunting instincts and these may lead your dog to chase wildlife.

Although all Labradors are energetic as puppies, adult working dogs may continue to be livelier and may pull on the lead. Labradors that

ABOVE: *You may want your dog as a family companion or to train him for a more specialized role.*

are bred to be shown tend to be rather more placid as youngsters and mellow as they grow up. On the other hand, show dogs tend to bark more than working dogs where this trait has been partially bred out of their breeding lines. Show-bred Labradors are often larger than gundogs. Your choice will depend on the kind of life you would like to have with your Labrador. Do you want to have an active or sporting life with him, or a more relaxed lifestyle? The more placid show Labrador may make a better therapy dog.

THE LABRADOR IS A NATURAL RETRIEVER

1 Keeping the dog sitting at your left-hand side, throw a dumb-bell.

2 Your dog's instincts will prompt him to chase the dumb-bell. Call him back to you.

3 In competition, the dog must present the dumb-bell to his handler.

4 The obedience-trained Lab will learn to stay with the handler out of sight.

OBEDIENCE TRAINING

As a breed, Labradors are generally very obedient and willing to please their owners. This means that with the right training and plenty of positive reinforcement, your Labrador can achieve a high level of obedience training. These traits mean that training is a fun activity for a Labrador. A good way to capitalize on this desire to obey you is to take your Labrador puppy to an obedience class. These classes will teach your pup the basics in the company of other puppies, so they will also give him opportunities to become socialized with other dogs. A once or twice-weekly class would be ideal. If you want to use your Labrador as a gundog, you may also wish to attend a retrieving class. You should ensure that your instructor is a specialist in this field. Alternatively, if you want to show your dog, you may want to take your young dog to training lessons that specialize in this area. Learning to stand correctly is very important for potential show dogs and you will need to teach your Labrador to stand or "stack." Stacking is when the dog stands squarely and still. To teach your puppy how to stand freely you need to practise so that he will stand correctly for a reasonable length of time. This can be done with treats; by gradually increasing the time he has to stand correctly to get his reward.

Obedience trials (which are sometimes part of general dog shows) are becoming increasingly popular as competitive activities for Labradors. There is usually a set programme for each part of the Trial and each competing dog is awarded points for his performance.

OBEDIENCE TITLES

There are plenty of titles to be won in the field of Obedience. In the UK, these titles include Companion Dog (CD), Utility Dog (UD), and Tracking Dog (TD), in ascending order of difficulty. In North America, the corresponding titles are: Companion Dog (CD), Companion Dog Excellent (CDX), Utility Dog (UD), Utility Dog Excellent (UDX),Tracking Dog (TD), and Tracking Dog Excellent (TDX).

POSITIVE REINFORCEMENT

No Labrador obedience training will be complete and successful without positive reinforcements. These are the praises, kind words and treats you give your dog if he does what you ask. A good way to reinforce this positive approach is to commend him with praise, along with a gentle tap on his head and a treat so that he knows that he has pleased you.

Keep treats in a pouch that is easy to access.

Agility training

Agility Training is becoming increasingly popular for many breeds of dog, including Labrador Retrievers. Owners and dogs can both get a lot of enjoyment from this competitive sport. Agility competitions take place over an obstacle course made up of jumps, tunnels, and walkways. Dogs and handlers work as teams, with the handler helping the dog to navigate the obstacles in the correct order. Some people do agility training just for fun, while others enjoy competing in agility trials. During the trials, dog and handler teams compete to see who can complete the obstacle course the fastest with the fewest mistakes.

ABOVE: *Your Labrador needs to be fit for Agility competitions.*

ABOVE: *The weaving poles are amongst the more difficult obstacles for your dog.*

However, it is important to remember that a Labrador needs to be at least a year old before he can participate in Agility training as this intense exertion could prove hazardous to a growing puppy. Once he is ready, however, your naturally obedient Labrador can excel at this kind of work.

TACKLING OBSTACLES

Most Agility courses contain several "contact" obstacles, including the A-frame, a dog walk, a see-saw, hurdles, a tyre, weaving poles, and the tunnel. "Contact" because your dog needs to touch specified parts of these obstacles with at least one paw. Although most dogs are perfectly happy to run through the tunnel, larger breeds like the Labrador Retriever can often find the weaving poles more challenging.

ABOVE: *Agility courses are made up from several different obstacles.*

Labradors usually start competing in Agility between the ages of one and two. As well as damaging his young bones, your pup could injure himself by jumping hurdles at too young an age. If you are in any doubt, consult your vet to see if your dog is ready to participate in Agility.

If you are hoping to take part in competitions, you can tailor your pup's early training with this in mind. Teaching him to obey the basic commands of sit, down, come, heel, and stay will be crucial to his success in Agility. Obedience classes will also teach him to concentrate even when he is surrounded by strange dogs and their owners. Once he is ready to begin his Agility training, you should look for a specialized Agility class in your area. These classes will give you and your pet the opportunity to try out an obstacle course without having to go to the trouble and expense of building your own obstacles.

Agility courses are made up from several "contact" obstacles. These include the A-frame, the see-saw, and the dog walk. The A-frame is a triangular-shaped walkway. Dogs must be able to walk up the steep incline and back down the other side. The dog walk works like a balance beam for dogs with a ramp at either end. The see-saw is just like one you would find at the playground. Your dog must learn to walk across it as it tips under his weight.

You can teach your dog to make contact at the correct points of the obstacles by leaving treats at these points. In this way, your dog gets the treats by putting his paw in the contact zone.

ABOVE: *The tyre is a more advanced challenge.*

ABOVE: *The hurdles*
BELOW: *The tunnel is often an easy task to master*

CONTACT POINTS

When you begin Agility training with your Labrador, make sure the obstacles are moved to the lowest position possible. Put your dog on a lead, and give him a specific command, such as "A-frame." Move quickly as you approach the obstacle, and lead him over it. You may need to use some extra special treats the first few times.

Gun dog training for Labradors

ABOVE: *The Labrador is born to retrieve – on land and in water.*

Labradors were originally bred to work as gundogs and training your dog for this purpose is a great way of channeling his natural bounce and energy. In the UK, the Gundog Club manages a graded training scheme for gundogs that was launched in 2006. Several thousand pet Labradors have now joined this scheme on their way to becoming fully-trained gundogs. The scheme is suitable for pets, working dogs and even show dogs. All true Labradors have the instinct to retrieve, and the training capitalizes on their natural instincts. Intelligent dogs like Labradors really enjoy this kind of challenging training and working together will help you form a great bond of mutual respect with your dog. Many people have no intention of using their dog in the field when they start gundog training, although they may change their minds when they see how this work comes so naturally to their Labrador.

In the first place, the best way to get your dog's training off to a good start is to join your local Labrador or Gun Dog club. The good news is that you don't need to be a landowner to

DUMMIES: TRADITIONAL VERSUS MODERN

The traditional gundog trainer's retrieving dummy is a one pound sawdust log. This is wrapped in plastic and then covered with canvas, often in a shade of aquamarine. An attached toggle makes for easier throwing. In America, most gundog trainers use moulded rubber or plastic dummies. These dummies are very light and easy to throw. Plastic dummies are often white. This means that they are easy to see against a background of earth, rock, and vegetation. As your dog becomes more advanced, you can use an orange dummy which is harder for the dog to see yet easy for you to spot. This will enable you to make more challenging retrieves without losing your equipment. Different shaped dummies are also on the market, while others leave a special scent.

Dummy with rope loop to enable throwing

Staghorn Whistles

Green canvas dummies filled with sand

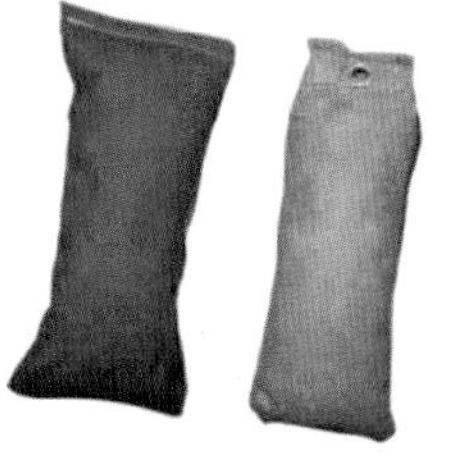

Dummy made with floatable material

ABOVE: *In the novice class, all the other dogs and owners will be beginners just like yourself.*

train a gundog. Most Gun Dog clubs will have access to a suitable piece of land, with differing terrain, where your dog can learn his new skills. The equipment you will need to get started is minimal – just a gundog slip-lead, and a one pound canvas training dummy. These can be found at country shows, gun shops, or on-line.

Retrieving

The lively and intelligent Labrador Retriever has a variety of in-born skills. As its name suggests, retrieving is one of them. But what if your Labrador just doesn't seem interested in playing fetch? Even though nearly all Labradors are born with an instinct to retrieve, it sometimes takes a little time and training to jumpstart this natural impulse. It might also be the case that, for a teething puppy who

ABOVE: *Start by using a toy to encourage the retrieve.*

ABOVE: *Give your dog plenty of praise when she brings back the dummy.*

is still cutting his adult teeth, picking up objects with his mouth might be uncomfortable. Most Labradors start to become more interested in retrieving at about six months old. Whether you are working with a puppy or an adult Labrador, the first step is to toss his toys and see if your Labrador shows an interest in running after them. It's more convenient to play this game in an enclosed area, like a hallway, where the dog can't avoid you after fetching the toy. When your dog brings the toy back to you, ask him to sit and gently take the toy from him. Then praise him and give him the toy back.

Once you have graduated from these first attempts to a training class, you and the other trainee handlers will be asked to make a line with your dogs. Dummies will then be thrown for you. Your job is to get your dog to wait until you are asked to retrieve the dummy. As soon as he does so, you should make him sit still in front of you, and gently take the dummy from him before giving him lots of praise. This training will continue until your dog can also retrieve hidden dummies, double dummies, and dummies floating on water. As his tuition becomes more advanced, your instructor may also encourage you to use hand signals to communicate with your dog.

ABOVE: *In time, your Labrador will progress to retrieving game.*

The versatile retriever

The Labrador Retriever may be most recognizable as a gun dog, but the breed's wonderful temperament - kind, intelligent, out-going, and relaxed - has also made the Labrador the world's favourite assistance dog.

GUIDE DOGS

The first guide dogs were trained at the end of World War I. Special dog training schools were set up in Germany, and German Shepherds were taught to help returning veterans who had been blinded in combat. The concept soon caught on in Britain and the United States, but Labradors were more popular in these countries. Labradors and Labrador crosses are now used as guide dogs for the blind throughout the world. Britain's famous charity, Guide Dogs for the Blind Association train several breeds as guide dogs, but Labradors and Labradors crossed with Golden Retrievers are the most easily recognized guide dogs. The charity now runs its own breeding programme, and produces between a thousand and

PUPPY PROFILING ASSESSMENT

Guide Dogs for the Blind now use a new technique Puppy Profiling Assessment (PPA) to grade their puppies. This is a unique tool that the charity uses to assess the temperament of their potential guide dogs before they place them on their famous puppy walking scheme. The assessment involves a series of special exercises undertaken by potential guide dogs to gauge their future temperament.

RIGHT: *Puppies are given an intensive programme of socialisation.*

fifteen hundred puppies each year. It costs around £50,000 to breed, train, and support a guide dog throughout its working life. The charity's breeding programme is so successful that at least 70 per cent of its puppies pass as fully trained guide dogs.

There are many reasons why Labradors make such successful guide dogs. Practically, they are medium-sized dogs who enjoy good general health and don't need a lot of specialist care or grooming. But their main strength is their fantastic temperament. Not only are they intelligent and easy to train, but they are also calm and unflappable. They are also loving and loyal and make fantastic bonds with their owners.

RIGHT: *The Labrador is intelligent and easy to train.*

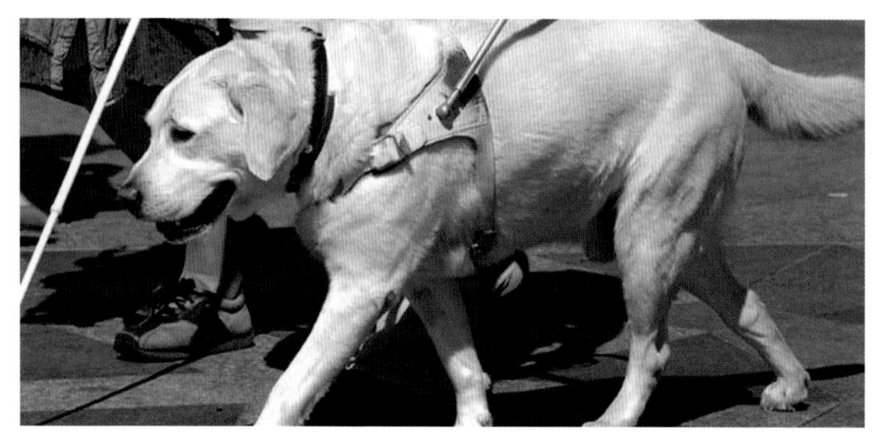

ABOVE: *A dog for the disabled makes everyday life easier for his owner.*

After their Puppy Profiling Assessments, the Labrador puppies are taken into the homes of volunteer puppy walkers. The charity funds the dogs' veterinary care and feeding costs. There are 3,500 volunteer puppy walkers in the UK. Each puppy walker cares for the trainee guide dog until it is twelve to fourteen months old. As well as looking after the puppy, the puppy walkers give the pups their basic training so that they can sit, go down, stay, come, and walk on the lead. They also expose their young dogs to as many different situations and environments as possible to build up their confidence and make them "bomb proof," walking them in country lanes and city streets.

Because of the high cost of guide dog training, and the very responsible nature of the guide dog's work, any unsuitable dogs are weeded out at this point. The puppies then undergo their first formal test at the age of nine to twelve months. If they pass, they then become trainee guide dogs.

The trainee dogs are then placed with guide dog trainers who give them the specialist training they need to support a blind person. They learn how to use a harness, how to cross the road and how to guide a blind person through various kinds of everyday obstacles.

The final stage of the dog's training is when the dog is matched with his blind owner. The pair then go into a period of intensive training together. Even when they go home together, the guide dog and his owner are supported by expert trainers from the Guide Dogs charity. After a working life of eight or nine years, guide dogs are usually retired and re-homed for a relaxing retirement.

HEARING DOGS FOR DEAF PEOPLE

Labradors also make excellent hearing dogs for deaf people. They are trained to alert deaf people to everyday sounds and danger signals in the home, work place or public buildings by tapping them with their paws or nudging with their noses. They work with both deaf children and adults and provide independence and companionship for their owners. The Hearing Dogs charity was first launched in 1982.

RIGHT: *The biddable Labrador adapts well to the role of hearing dog.*

ASSISTANCE DOGS

Being an assistance dog is a new role for the Labrador, but one that he seems made for with his calm, confident and obedient character. Assistance dogs can be trained to work with adults with different disabilities and sometimes quite complex needs. Specially-trained assistance Labradors can offer greater independence through practical support. They can pick up dropped items, open doors, help with dressing and undressing, and even empty the washing machine. Disabled children can also benefit from having an assistance dog. The practical support that the dog gives them helps them towards confidence and independence.

LABRADORS AS THERAPY DOGS

With their calm and affectionate natures, Labrador Retrievers can be trained to make wonderful therapy dogs. These sociable dogs willingly submit to be handled, cuddled and petted by strangers in often quite stressful surroundings such as hospitals, schools, and nursing homes. Patients really look forward to these visits because therapy dogs provide unconditional affection, comfort, and entertainment when they need it most, chasing away boredom and depression. Some of the things that make Labradors especially good in this role are their trainability and obedience. For example, one of most important commands for a therapy dog is "leave it!" so that they don't pick up dropped pills or food. Not only do sick and elderly people cheer up around therapy dogs, but children can be encouraged to get over a fear of dogs by patting and cuddling this patient and soft-hearted breed.

RIGHT *The patient and soft-hearted Labrador makes a wonderful therapy dog.*

POLICE AND ARMY LABRADORS

Labradors have been used by the police, army and border forces for many years. In 1938 two specially trained black Labradors were introduced to the Metropolitan Police as general patrol, tracker and utility dogs. Their role within the police has now been greatly extended to include sniffer dogs, who are trained to find drugs, explosives and even cadavers. Despite their reputation for being soft and gentle, Labradors are also trained for personal protection and criminal apprehension duties, where a good degree of controlled aggression is required. Police dogs undergo at least eight to ten weeks of intensive training, which usually starts at the age of one to eighteen months. This training uses a system of praise and reward and the dogs form a close bond with their handlers. This training is refreshed throughout their working lives which may last for up to eight years. When Police Labradors are retired, they usually stay with their handlers as pets. Although black Labradors seem to be the favourite colour for police work, all three colours of the breed are used.

6 LABRADOR HEALTH ISSUES

Generally speaking, Labradors are robustly healthy dogs that live ten to fourteen years and sometimes longer. Although (as in many breeds of dog) there are a number of health conditions that have been identified within the breed, many of these can be avoided by health screening.

But even the healthiest dogs can have minor accidents and illnesses and you need to find a good vet to take care of your Labrador's general health needs.

FINDING A VET

Ideally you should decide which vet you plan on using before you pick up your Labrador puppy. Ask your friends which vets they recommend and if possible, take the time to visit the clinic and look around. You may also want to find out when your vet graduated. Veterinarians that graduated many years ago may be experienced but may not be as up to date on medical knowledge and technology as recent graduates while vets that have graduated more recently may have a lot of the latest information but little hands on experience. You also need to ascertain if the vet's office hours will fit your schedule and if they handle emergencies after hours. You should also consider insuring your puppy as veterinary care becomes increasingly expensive. If you are concerned about your dog, take him to see your vet as soon as possible. A stitch in time saves nine!

BELOW: *The Labrador is an active healthy breed requiring fewer visits to the vets.*

Common Labrador health problems

Anal glands All dogs have a pair of small sacs on either side of their anus. These anal glands produce a smelly, yellowish-gray to brownish pasty material, which is usually expelled when he defecates. Anal gland problems happen when the sacs become inflamed, impacted, infected, irritated, abscessed or affected by tumours. Dogs with anal sac problems can't properly eliminate the material that their glands normally produce. This causes lots of itchiness, pain and general discomfort. Unfortunately, anal sac problems are fairly common in domestic dogs. The reasons for this are not fully understood, but several factors have been suggested, including obesity, bouts of diarrhoea, poor anal muscle tone, and poor diet.

Arthritis affects some older Labradors. Arthritis is the inflammation of one or more joints. It can be caused by traumatic injuries, physical deformities, joint infections, genetic predispositions, or problems with the immune system. Arthritis is painful, progressive and usually permanent. It can lead to joint deformities, lameness, stiffness and loss of normal joint function. There are a number of things that owners can do to help their arthritic dogs lead full and fairly pain-free lives. These include weight management (especially important for obesity-prone Labradors), dietary and lifestyle changes, surgical procedures and medications and supplements that provide pain relief. These treatments may also delay further joint damage.

ABOVE: *Regular exercise will help to keep your dog fit and healthy.*

Fits and seizures can occur in dogs of any age, sex or breed. In young dogs, most dog fits are epileptic seizures, seizures caused by toxins, metabolic disorders or abnormalities. In older dogs seizures are sometimes caused by brain tumours. Puppies infested with worms can also fit, or if they have a reaction to their vaccinations. Most fits will be preceded by a pattern of altered behaviour. This may include staring into space, agitation, nervousness, restlessness, vocalization, clinginess, seeking seclusion, or confusion. The fit itself may cause the dog to show some of the following symptoms: weakness, loss of awareness, trembling, rigidity, stopping breathing (for between 5 and 30 seconds), muscle twitching (especially in the face), chewing, frenzied barking, snapping, temporary blindness, vomiting, drooling, urination/defecation, collapse, or loss of consciousness. During the fit, you should not interfere, but make sure that your dog does not hurt himself. Once the fit is over, the dog will probably feel weak, wobbly and confused. If your dog has another fit you should take him to your vet.

Heatstroke is an elevation of a dog's core body temperature to intolerable levels. It is usually due to external factors (such as a dog being left in a hot car). Dogs don't tolerate high temperatures at all well because they don't sweat. Dogs with heat stroke become increasingly restless and uncomfortable as their temperature rises. They pant, have trouble breathing and become weak. Eventually, they lie down and slip into a coma. By this point, death is imminent unless the dog receives immediate aggressive medical attention.

Ear Care Your Labrador's ears need regular care and checking to make sure that they keep clean and infection free.

A dog's ears can become irritated for many reasons. Parasites can cause unbearable ear irritation. Fleas and mange mites can often settle in ears, causing hair loss, itchiness and inflammation. They can also contribute to waxy build up in the ear canal. Foreign objects such as ticks, seeds, grass seeds and other plant material can work their way down the outer ear canal and cause pain and inflammation. Weather extremes may also contribute to ear problems. Moisture and heat create a rich habitat for bacterial proliferation, and icy weather can cause frostbite. Allergies are also often associated with ear discomfort. Reactions can be caused by food, particles, or parasites, especially fleas. Ear infections are caused by yeasts and bacteria and outer ear infections can move into the middle and inner ear.

If your Labrador keeps shaking his head, or one ear is hanging lower than the other, you should take him to the vet for checking. Whatever the problem, it is important to sort this out as secondary ear problems can develop if the underlying cause is not addressed. If your Labrador loves swimming, it's a good idea to dry the external part of his ears.

ABOVE: *Try to keep an injured dog quiet until you can get treatment.*

PROBLEM PARASITES

Fleas are small, flat, wingless, blood-sucking insects that are an irritation to dogs and their owners alike. They can also can carry and transmit serious diseases and other parasites (such as tapeworms). They are also the leading cause of skin problems in domestic dogs. Dogs become infested if good flea prevention isn't followed. Fortunately, there are many things that dog owners can do to keep fleas under control. Some dogs can have a severe reaction to flea bites (flea dermatitis or eczema). If you think that you have found flea debris in your dog's coat, collect some of the black grit from the coat and put it on a white tissue. If the black grit goes blood-coloured when you wet it, your dog has fleas.

Ticks are tiny parasites that feed on the blood of their hosts. They are usually found in sheep and cattle but can also affect domestic dogs in the summer months. They can carry and transmit bacterial organisms that cause infectious diseases - such as the bacteria that cause Lymes disease. Ticks can be removed by using flea-control remedies that are also designed to remove ticks. Other methods involve removing the tick with special forceps, making sure you grasp the head. But if you don't manage to remove the tick's mouth parts, the bite can become infected.

Roundworms are the most common internal parasites of dogs. Most puppies have some roundworm infection. Adult roundworms spend most of their lives in the dog's stomach and small intestine. Dogs become infected when they swallow roundworm eggs or eat infected rodents. Roundworms can cause stomach ache, vomiting, diarrhoea, and coughing. Infected dogs develop a dull coat, distended abdomen and stunted growth. Dogs should be regularly wormed to control this problem.

Tapeworms are parasites that live inside a dog's small intestine. They can range from less than one inch to several feet in length. They are transmitted by fleas and lice. Tapeworms bury into the sensitive lining of a dog's intestine, feeding on blood and sucking up essential nutrients. Adult tapeworms develop egg packets, which eventually break off and are passed out in the dog's faeces. Owners may see tapeworm segments crawling around their dog's rear end. They look like grains of rice. Modern tapeworm treatments are very effective and your vet will advise on how often you should treat your dog.

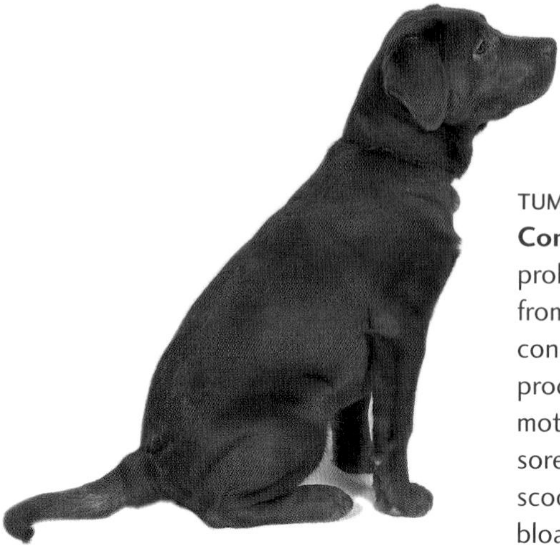

Lice are small insects, averaging between 1.5 to 4 millimeters in length. Usually, they can be seen by the naked eye. They live for about four weeks. Their eggs (nits) can look like scurf on a dog's coat. They can be either biting or sucking lice. Lice are uncommon in clean, healthy, well-fed and well-maintained companion dogs and tend to thrive mostly on debilitated dogs that are old, run-down, malnourished or poorly cared for.

TUMMY TROUBLE

Constipation often reflects dietary problems but affects many Labradors from time-to-time. Symptoms of constipation can include non-productive straining, hard and dry motions, mucus from the anus, pain, soreness or swelling in the anal area, scooting, lack of appetite, abdominal bloating or discomfort, vomiting, weight loss, depression, and lethargy. While mild constipation usually resolves itself, severe constipation can be a medical emergency and should be treated very quickly.

ABOVE: *Get into the habit of checking your dog's feet after walks.*

Middle-aged and older dogs tend to be more prone to constipation, as normal bowel activity tends to decrease with age. Dogs that do not drink enough water also tend to become constipated. Constipation is sometimes treated with laxatives to draw water into the intestines and soften the faeces. Enemas can also be used to evacuate the bowel.

Another potential treatment option is adding milk to the dog's diet. The lactose in milk is difficult for dogs to digest and often causes diarrhoea. Olive or mineral oils are also used. If the attack goes on for longer than a day, you should contact your vet as your dog may have some kind of blockage. Labradors do have a tendency to swallow toys, balls and other household objects!

Diarrhoea is usually a symptom of some underlying medical condition rather than an illness in itself, but it requires prompt attention and treatment. It is usually acute (it comes and quickly and then goes away) but can be chronic (it comes on slowly and lasts for a long time). Unless the underlying cause is diagnosed and resolved, this unpleasant condition can keep coming and going.

To avoid diarrhoea, owners should feed their Labrador with a high quality diet and try to prevent their dogs eating rubbish, contaminated foods, or non-edible items (such as plastic or balls). You should check your dog closely when he has diarrhoea. You should give him a solution of glucose and water to drink to make sure that he doesn't dehydrate. Fast him for 24 hours and then start to feed him with an easy-to-digest diet, chicken, or fish. If he doesn't improve quite quickly, you should take him to your vet.

Lameness is another of those canine conditions that can occur for a whole range of reasons. Labradors can go lame for many reasons. The most common causes are found in the foot itself so you should check this first for cuts, cracks, dried mud between the pads, thistles or swelling. Check the nails have not been damaged or that the nailbed is not infected. Sores between the pads can also cause lameness. If you find a foreign body in the paw, remove it and clean the foot with warm antiseptic water. In puppies, lameness can be caused by growing pains in the long bones.

If you can't find anything wrong in the paw, check further up the dog's leg. You should feel for any swellings, lumps or cuts. Feel the opposite leg and compare the shape and size. You should also find out if there is any difference in the heat of the legs; bend the joints and move the leg. The dog may or may not flinch when you touch the injury.

Some dogs will be lame one day and, after resting overnight, will be completely sound the next. However, if the cause of your dog's lameness is still undetected and has not improved after two days, you should take him to your vet.

ABOVE: *If your dog is lame for two days or more see your vet.*

ABOVE: *If you are worried about your Labrador's condition, seek veterinary advice.*

EYE PROBLEMS

Those gentle Labrador eyes that melt the hearts of their human companions are also often susceptible to several problems that can result in blindness. Unfortunately, there are several causes of vision loss associated with this breed of dog. There are three main causes of blindness in Labradors. Retinal dysplasia is where the layers of retinal tissue separate which causes the blood supply to be cut off to healthy tissue. Unfortunately, there is no cure for this condition, which can strike at any age. PRA (or progressive retinal atrophy) is a condition where the blood vessels to the retina gradually stop working. Starved of oxygen and nutrients, the retina slowly dies. Labradors are also susceptible to cataracts, but these can be surgically removed.

LEFT: *If you exercise your dog over sheep pastures, he risks contracting tapeworms.*

Hereditary Labrador diseases

Although Labradors are mostly happy and healthy, the breed is prone to several hereditary diseases. However, responsible breeders do not breed from dogs afflicted with these conditions, so there is every chance that your puppy will not be a carrier of any of them.

Hip dysplasia is a serious condition that affects several breeds of dog, but Labradors (especially larger dogs) seem especially prone to it. This degenerative condition affects the hip joint of the hind legs and can be crippling. A puppy can be born with seemingly normal hips, but the symptoms of the condition can appear as he matures. All responsible Labrador breeders have their breeding animals checked for signs of the condition, even if they are breeding from their own pets. When Labrador puppies are offered for sale, dogs from reputable breeders will be described as "hip scored." This means that their parents' hip joints have been x-rayed to determine how likely it is that they

will develop dysplasia. Expert vets then "score" the x-rayed joint to see how "normal" it is. Every deviation from a perfect hip joint gets points, so a score of zero is perfect, while a score of fifty is very bad. The points for each hip are then added together so that the dog is awarded an overall score.

Shoulder osteochondrosis
As many as five per cent of all Labrador Retrievers will be affected by this debilitating condition. Osteochondrosis is a disease of the shoulder joint cartilage, and most Labradors that suffer from the condition are affected in both shoulders. The condition occurs when the shoulder cartilage becomes thickened and diseased, and eventually separates from the underlying bone. The resulting flap of loose cartilage may break off and float around within the joint. Painful in itself, it can also lead to the development of crippling arthritis. Affected dogs can become lame and in severe cases, permanently disabled. Rest can have some positive effect, but a permanent surgical cure is required in advanced cases.

PRA blindness Progressive Retinal Atrophy is also a hereditary condition in Labradors. The good news is that the potentially faulty carrier gene for this condition has now been identified. A simple DNA test, the Optigen test, can determine if a dog has the two faulty genes that mean that he will inevitable suffer PRA blindness. This is important information for breeders, as puppies born to two "clear" parents can never contract the disease.

Summary

The Labrador Retriever has not become the most popular dog in the United States and Great Britain by accident. We are charmed by his easygoing and loveable temperament, his intelligence and his unfussy hardiness. Versatile to a fault, a Labrador can adapt himself to almost any home or family. All he needs is a little health care, a good diet, exercise and most of all, our love.